Pants Attack!

Clive Gifford

Illustrated by Gemma Silcox

Letts

Rick stayed late after school.
It was dark when he got home to his block of flats.
There was a full moon sticking out of the black night sky.
Rick kicked the ground.
A full moon was bad luck for him.

"On a night, when
a full moon shines,"
he said out loud,
"old, thrown-away clothes
sometimes come alive."

Rick felt a bit sick.
He did not want
to go back home.

2

Tonight, who knows what
just might attack!

These are all words of things which might frighten some people. Can you draw a line from each word to match its picture?

lion

ghost

spider

night

witch

bats

snake

wolf

3

"Can we stay up all night and have **lots** of snacks?"
Rick asked Nicki, his babysitter.
"No, Rick, it is time for bed,"
said Nicki.

Rick checked
the clock.
It was five
to eight.

"Shall I tuck you in?" asked
Nicki. Rick shook his head
and went off to bed.

He picked up his backpack
and put it by the bedroom door.
Rick locked the door. He checked the lock twice.
He flicked the light off and tucked up in bed.
With luck he would fall asleep and all would be fine.

4

All the children whose names start with letters from A to M wear orange pants. All the kids whose names start with letters from N to Z wear purple. Write orange or purple next to each name.

Jill _____

Ollie _____

Steve _____

Emma _____

Rick _____

Wendy _____

Harry _____

Alan _____

Colin _____

Tim _____

Donna _____

Jim _____

Sally _____

Neil _____

Kelly _____

Robert _____

The clock struck nine,
but Rick was still not asleep.
TICK-TOCK went the clock.
TICK-TOCK, TICK-TOCK.
Rick tried to count all the ticks
the clock made.
He hoped it would make him tired.
It worked!

By ten o'clock,
Rick was fast
asleep.

But behind Rick's clothes rack
lay an old sack. At midnight,
something started to
move in the sack. It was
small. It was black.
It began to unpack. It slid out
of the sack and past Rick's black mac.
And it began to cackle as it crawled past the rack.

Can you match the times on the clocks with the words which describe them?

a quarter to one

nine o'clock

five o'clock

ten past two

half past ten

ten to three

half past four

a quarter past five

Rick woke up. He thought he heard a sound.
But now, there was just the clock going TICK-TOCK.
Maybe the sound had been ants in the floor cracks.
Or it might have been a flock of ducks
outside going "quack".

"Hello Rick!"
Rick turned
around. The
back of his neck
went all prickly
with sweat.

An old
pair of Rick's
underpants
stood on his bed.

"H..h..how did you
get in?
Did you pick the lock?

"No, I was here all the
time in a sack at the bac
of your clothes rack."

8

Many words contain smaller words hiding inside them. Can you seek out smaller words with two or more letters in each?

bed   _____

sock   _____

line   _____

wall   _____

wrong   _____

flick   _____

house   _____

clock   _____

crack   _____

flat   _____

"Remember, Rick," said the pants,
"how we used to have fun?"
When it came to pairs of pants,
I was your number one.
I was the first thing you
would pack in your holiday
backpack. But then the fun
stopped," said the pants.
They **sagged**
and went a little slack.
"You chucked me away
and put me in your old
clothes sack."

"I got too big for you," said
Rick. "It was just bad luck."

"No, the bad luck is yours,
Rick," said the pants.
"I have not been unpacked
for a long, long time.
But now I am unpacked, I plan
to **attack!**"

Here are things Rick packs in his backpack when he goes on holiday. Can you write them down in order from the shortest to the longest word?

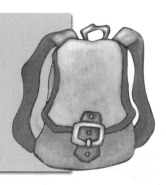

sunglasses

coat

sandals

_____

_____

_____

hat

_____

spade

_____

sun cream

bucket

_____

Rick rocked back in shock as the pants attacked.
The pants **kicked** and flicked Rick's toys off the shelf.
They smacked Rick's model car off the desk.
Rick ducked as his car flew by.
It smacked into the wall and cracked in two.

The pants then **mucked** up his hair.
And chucked his clothes in the air.
The pants **cracked** his best mug.
And knocked books off his desk.

Then, they **whacked** his clock onto the floor.

12

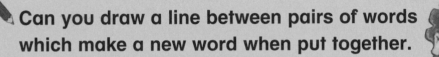

Can you draw a line between pairs of words which make a new word when put together.

under	stick
arm	chair
back	print
lip	master
neck	pants
some	times
head	lace
finger	pack

13

As the pants attacked, Rick's mind clicked.
"It is time for me to **fight back!**"

He had once read a poem, that stopped bad pants in their tracks.

Rick shut his eyes as he shouted out the words.

"Underpants, underpants go away you are bad pants, you are mad pants. You must not stay.

I have grown up. You are too small for me. Underpants, underpants, now you must flee."

Rick opened his eyes.
The pants had gone.
"Wow, the poem worked.
What a slick trick!"

Rick wrote all about what happened when the pants attacked, but he tore up the piece of paper by mistake. Can you match the pieces of paper to make eight whole sentences?

It was dark when

I was scared

Nicki told me

I counted the

My old black pants

The pants were

I said a poem

My lucky socks

to go home.

saved me just in time.

but it did not work.

I left school.

angry with me.

woke me up.

ticks of the clock.

to go to bed.

"Yes, slick indeed," mocked the pants. They were behind Rick's back.

"The poem you picked was just a trick! And now," said the pants, "it is time you got a smack."

"But you have already mucked up my hair and whacked my toys," cried Rick.

"Oh, that was just a small rant," said the pants. "That was not a real Pants Attack."

Rick felt sick. He was out of luck.

The pants began to cackle as they got ready to attack.

But they didn't see the socks leap out of Rick's backpack.

All the clothes in this wardrobe need their names to be spelt correctly. See if you put the letters in the right order and write out the word.

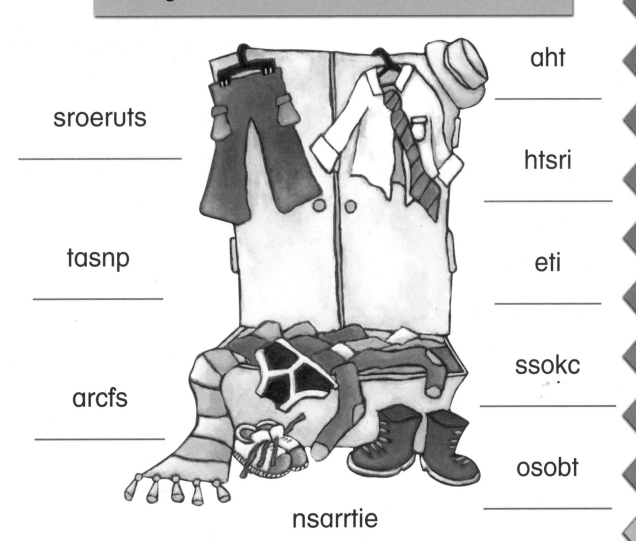

aht

_____

sroeruts

_____

htsri

_____

tasnp

_____

eti

_____

ssokc

_____

arcfs

_____

osobt

_____

nsarrtie

_____

"**M**y lucky socks!" cried Rick as the socks attacked the pants. The socks kicked and struck and smacked the pants.

"That's for scaring Rick sick," said the socks as they whacked.

"Take that you bad pants!
    And that!
        And that!"

One sock picked up a stick, while the other sock kicked. The pants were soon stuck on the end of the stick.

"Rick, say knickers three times," said one of the socks. "Are you mucking around? Is this a trick?"
"No, do it quick, Rick, before the pants break the stick."

18

The Rocking Socks pop band cannot sing the letter **s**. Can you add the missing letters to complete their song?

We are the Rocking ock .

And thi i our ong.

We like to ing and play mu ic all day long.

Lefty i on the drum kit.

Righty ings along.

At the end of the ong, Lefty hit a big gong.

"Knickers," said Rick.
The pants bucked and rocked on the end of the stick. "Knickers," said Rick for the second time.
"Do not say it again!" ranted the pants.
"**KNICKERS!**" cried Rick.

There was a loud
crack
and the pants went slack.
They slid off the stick and
lay still on the floor.

"It is all over Rick," said the socks.
You can go back to sleep.
"We will stick the pants in a sack
and chuck them away.
Those pants will not come back to attack."
"Wow! Thanks," said Rick.
"My lucky socks rock!"

Do you think you know the story of Rick and how his old pants attacked him? See if you can answer all these questions.

 | Where had Rick been before he came home?

_____

 2 What was the name of Rick's babysitter?

_____

 3 Did Rick lock the door or put his backpack by the door first?

_____

4 At what time do we know Rick was asleep?

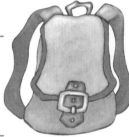

_____

5 What birds did Rick think might have made the sound that woke him up?

_____

 6 What flew past Rick and made him duck?

_____

Answers

Page 3

 lion   witch

 ghost   bats

 spider   snake

 night   wolf

Page 5

Orange

Jill	Colin
Emma	Donna
Harry	Jim
Alan	Kelly

Purple

Ollie	Tim
Steve	Sally
Rick	Neil
Wendy	Robert

Page 7

 nine o'clock   a quarter past five

 five o'clock   a quarter to one

 half past four   ten past two

 half past ten   ten to three

Page 9

bed – be	flick – lick
sock – so	house – use
line – in	clock – lock
wall – all	crack – rack
wrong – on	flat – at

Page 11

hat
coat
spade
bucket
sandals
sun cream
sunglasses

Page 13

underpants

armchair

backpack

lipstick

necklace

sometimes

headmaster

fingerprint

Page 15

It was dark when I left school.

I was scared to go home.

Nicki told me to go to bed.

I counted the ticks of the clock.

My old black pants woke me up.

The pants were angry with me.

I said a poem but it did not work.

My lucky socks saved me just in time.

Page 17

trousers

pants

scarf

trainers

hat

shirt

tie

socks

boots

Page 19

We are the Rocking **S**ock**s**.

And thi**s** i**s** our **s**ong.

We like to **s**ing and play mu**s**ic all day long.

Lefty i**s** on the drum kit.

Righty **s**ings along.

At the end of the **s**ong, Lefty hit**s** a big gong.

Page 21

1 School

2 Nicki

3 Put his backpack by the door.

4 Ten o'clock

5 Ducks

6 His model car

Published 2004

10 9 8 7 6 5 4 3 2

Letts Educational, The Chiswick Centre,
414 Chiswick High Road, London W4 5TF
Tel 020 8996 3333   Fax 020 8996 8390
Email mail@lettsed.co.uk
www.letts-education.com

Text, design and illustrations © Letts Educational Ltd 2004

Book Concept, Development and Series Editor:
Helen Jacobs, Publishing Director
Author: Clive Gifford
Book Design: Sandra Perry
Illustrations: Gemma Silcox

Letts Educational Limited is a division of Granada Learning.
Part of Granada plc.
British Library Cataloguing in Publication Data

A CIP record for this book is available from the British Library.

ISBN 1 84315 420 X

Printed in Italy

Colour reproduction by PDQ Digital Media Limited, Bungay, Suffolk